The Surface of Last Scattering

The Surface
of
Last Scattering

Gray Jacobik

Winner of the 1998 X. J. Kennedy Poetry Prize

Texas Review Press
Huntsville, Texas

FIRST EDITION, 1999

Requests for permission to reproduce material from this work should be sent to:

Permissions
Texas Review Press
English Department
Sam Houston State University
Huntsville, TX 77341-2146

Acknowledgments

My thanks to the following publications where the following poems first appeared:

The Kenyon Review for "Etymology," *The American Voice* for "Demeter in November," *The Prose Poem* for "A Little Charade," *Tar River Poetry* for "Death is a Material Flower," *LUNA* for "The Nap" and "Apples," *Manzanita Quarterly* for "Faith," *Poet Lore* for "The Sphere" (under the title "Window With A Dozen Small Frames"), *Ploughshares* for "The Ideal," *Sycamore Review* for "The Disclosure," *Ontario Review* for "Perspectives," "Pregnant," and "The Girls of Cork City."

My gratitude, as well, to James and Susan Finnegan and The Brickwalk Poets of West Hartford for weekly support and careful, critical readings of a number of these poems, and to Joan Seliger Sidney and Brad Davis who worked with me during my sabbatic leave. I owe a special debt to Mary Ann Larkin, who read this manuscript in its entirety and made many wise suggestions for revisions. Most especially, I am thankful to Robert Cording for his astute and sensitive comments, without which these poems would be less well formed than they are. And I am deeply grateful to Bruce Gregory, my first and wisest reader.

Library of Congress Cataloging-in-Publication Data

Jacobik, Gray
    The surface of last scattering / Gray Jacobik
        p.   cm. — (The X. J. Kennedy poetry prize)
    ISBN 1-881515-20-6 (paper)
    I. Title   II. Series
PS3560.A249S85   1999
811'.54—dc21   99-19301
                              CIP

For Jamie and Christianne

Table of Contents

Whole Speech > 1

The Girls of Cork City > 2

Demeter in November > 4

Psyche > 5

Emily > 6

The Nap > 7

The Sphere > 8

Faith > 10

The End > 11

The Speaker > 13

Apples > 14

Leaving Lovers > 16

Vermeer > 17

Death is a Material Flower > 19

*"Every Man Whose Soul Is Not A
    Clod Hath Visions"* > 20

The Astronomer's Wife > 22

In Brightest Light > 23

West Of Tuscon > 25

The Disclosure > 26

Memory of Longing > 27

Armageddon > 28

Disorders > 30

Silver Lotus, Golden Lotus > 31

11:00 A.M. > 32

Making Love > 34

Two Friends of Mine > 36

Snowmelt > 37

Etymology > 39

Night Work > 40

Genius > 41

The Ideal > 42

Bittersweet > 43

A Little Charade > 45

Privacy > 46

The Beloved's Body > 47

Sleeping In > 48

Perspective > 49

Pregnant > 50

Ramelli's Reading Wheel > 51

Irish Holiday > 53

Stardust > 54

Under the Sign of Walt Whitman > 56

Irises > 57

The Wind > 59

Bones > 60

A West Cork Suite > 62

We can see no further back in time than to the moment matter and radiation separated—

—The Surface of Last Scattering

"Too many lives are needed to make just one."

—Eugenio Montale

Whole Speech

What does it mean to speak with one's whole being?
How shape a full-bodied intelligent speaking
for an open-hearted listening? The way, this morning,
I spoke to the hemlock I stood under—hemlock
in its snow-shroud and sunlit-glitter above two
rimmed circles where deer, sleeping, left the impress
of themselves. I spoke to the raspberry cane,
frost-glazed or coated with that ashy dust it wears
when leaf bare. I spoke to the dogs as they played
like two child ruffians, then stopped to chew
the ice clumps from their splayed paws, but how
to say what this speaking consists of? Say it to you,
a stranger? Something occurs in the center of my body
that is not breathing, perhaps not physical, and an
immense silence hovers, or flaps off like a startled crow.
The gardens at Arles VanGogh painted so lavishly
in greens and yellow-greens, blues and golds
are whole acts of attention that translate easily
into other acts of attention, yet I cannot say what
calls forth this speaking. I walked home uphill
behind two young girls who were whispering
and giggling. Two heads leaning together,
hair fanning around their upper backs, bright
strands of it against one red and one blue jacket,
ease and affection, a prankish conspiratorial air.
I knew them, or was them, or had been them,
and so whole being addressed them, although
nothing was said. Their voices were songs birds
sometimes lend the young, the way, at times,
birds borrow the cries of children to say what their
voices cannot say. But where does this leave you and me?

The Girls Of Cork City

One Saturday evening in late June,
   beautiful girls tottered along
      in high platform shoes,
         bare of leg, short of skirt, sleeveless.

They were holding themselves
   because, quite possibly, they were cold,
      but this crossing of arms over breasts
         gave each a contradictory look,

for they were offering themselves up
   for the delectation of others
      and withholding themselves,
         an ambivalent gesture, unreserved

from the waist down, reticent
   from the waist up, walking alone
      or in pairs, off to the pubs and clubs
         and chippers, off to the films.

Discharged from a father's Renault,
   three friends all in halter-tops,
      and unbelievably, pedal-pushers,
         were beside themselves with glee

searching Oliver Plunkett Street
   for the liveliest commotion
      spilling itself out-of-doors.
         Like puffs on a breeze they floated . . . .

Others trotted along in outfits
   that no doubt worked before
      their long bedroom mirrors,
         but now, with the leering leaning

against walls, skirts and blouses shrunk
   under the collapse of showy intentions.
      Still, these girls did not stay home
         in their close-by suburbs or villages

malingering as some late adolescents do
   who have begun to doubt life will ever
      move off-center. One could see
         how soon to wives and mothers all

their very bodies bore them
   in those ridiculous shoes; chilled,
      bone-thin, preparing for the long race
         each generation races.

Demeter In November

She dwells where my cries cannot reach her,
while the evidence of her presence—berries, the ruined beds—
is strewn about, inescapable. The sky's longer light, her warmth,
the abiding ease we lavish our spirits in for months,
ripped from me. I am frozen. If I could slay her husband,
whose strength matches my own, I am no longer sure I would.
He is detestable, the goat-faced autocrat of a dismal realm,
yet she is devoted to him—his ridicule feeds something in her.
What moves her toward him? Is it the power of his thrusts?
Were those seeds she swallowed the seeds of death, so Eros
and Thanatos combine in her flesh? By July, I catch her looking
out to sea, by August her gaze turns inward, her moods change.
Yes, she pines for him, although I can still engage her,
still draw forth her laughter, her pleasure in the simplest things.
Delight is her first gift, ease her natural grace. Those first days
of her return, March, and we plan a thousand schemes and walk
near and far, mother and daughter, cherished friends, gathering,
inspecting, completing our setting-out tasks. Festival music
accompanies us and the sound of brooks and cataracts,
full-throated birds at the peak of their industry. Then shrubs
and trees bloom and each flower takes its mandated turn.
Life burgeons in us, burgeons *from* us, the sweet fecundity of mirth,
the fields, and the field of our bodies, the corn green-sprouting
across furrowed plains. But now I sit in dark, sleep in cold,
strive not to think, to weep. A daughter's destiny cannot be
a mother's destiny, yet Persephone will return to me,
will embrace me, her full woman's breasts against my breasts.

Psyche

Bowsprit of aspiration that requires us to move,
keep moving and never gaze at the ocean for long
dazzled by its roiling light, that spiraling spinning
impulse that wakes up in us each morning with
our first cup of tea or coffee, will of the world
to pluck its own fruit, a promise made real
with steps taken, phone calls made, books read
and digested the way a mole digests the cricket
it brings into its burrow, the body's best posture,
best rhythm rocking deep in the bones, the grace
of a good day's worthy blessings, soft kumquat
and hard walnut of tasks accomplished, pliable
couch of long complex dreams, clear springs
that trickle out of damp leaves beside mosses that,
if touched, would disappear, that curve we would
hold in the cup of our palm and stroke like the head
of a kitten, oh psyche, oh mind, unknowable that
goes before us into the hours and yards and city
streets, ghost of wishes, mythic house we sweep
the rooms of, climb the stairs of, pray in the corners of,
where do you come from? How can we shape you?
How sustain you beyond this our small portion?

Emily

I spent my birthday with a woman who might
    have been myself thirty years ago, myself
    without the early tragedies. Her thirst for

experience, her talent for using it, I know as clearly
    as, after a long day, I know the small of my back.
    Her sweetness is the sweetness that once held me

captive, that gained me lovers, interviews, access,
    that cost me the silver anguish that grows from
    trusting too much. Part of her is a fawn in the forest,

half-awake, half-asleep, one ear cocked for the rustle
    of her mother, the other for the rush of a riotous
    stream. And in her, too, the rasp and heft of intense

claims—those of the flesh and spirit that are turning
    her desires into flashes as she explodes out
    beyond herself to move across fields and cities

the eye devours, touch names. Love, Tsvetayeva tells us,
    is a flower flooded with blood. I wish Emily
    that flower, that blood, and beg no caution

of her, urge no restraint. She senses even now,
    at twenty-two, all years garner sorrows—this
    knowledge glistens in her eyes as she turns to go.

The Nap

1

Emptiness ascends through the afternoon—
a long mild afternoon of amber light,
for the light falls filtered through the dark pines,
and the lower deciduous leaves are bright
and newly-born. Such music as there would be
would not be clearly heard, but as at a distance,
across water, or drifting up from a low valley,
the broken vibrations adding to the emptiness
that quickens with memories of similar afternoons
when we slept in a soft light, lake water lapping the pier.

2

Difficult, too, not to deflect this vacancy
with the pleasures of the body—dear friend,
old betrayer, companionable burden,
source of transport—and of pain.
Yet we release—as if they were two kites
wavering in a blue sky—the impelling forces
of memory and sensation. Easier and more
pleasant, while life brims poignant and tart,
to let enormity amplify without distraction.

3

Blankness, vacuity, void, enlarging and scattering
until there seems to be no shred of existence,
at least none where impressions and thoughts
flood a reputed self reputedly thinking—
emptiness now a rip in the fabric, a gash
in the painting, the silence that makes music
possible. Heavy body, tempered body, body
of repose that vanishes in radiance, we sleep
as if sleep were a dryad who, tumbling from trees,
envies the passion and privilege of being human.

The Sphere

Their first time they were wonderfully tender
    toward one another, so tenderness moved
    still deeper into the core of each. A cottage

bed, mattress over a plywood platform nailed
    to thick log legs. Torn patchwork quilt.
    Near the window with a dozen small panes,

a blooming apple tree, lichen-embroidered.
    Spilling further down the slope to Fiery Run,
    a neglected orchard, rolling hills for another

six miles westward, then the greening Shenandoahs.
    The trees wavered with bees, and as far as
    they could see, a lacework of blossoms, old bark,

new green leaves like little licks of fire, grass, and the
    white airy seedpods of dandelion. They kissed,
    moved apart, kissed again, renewing and enlarging

their sensations until they were pure creatures, neither
    human nor other, but beyond themselves. The lichen,
    silver when they first arrived, turned turquoise, then

greyish-green. Because such a day changes one forever—
    when they rose and dressed and returned to the city,
    then drove back to their apartments, one northward,

another eastward—it seemed as if each, through the days
    to come, carried a glass sphere near the center
    of the body, a sphere filled with a liquid metal

like mercury that splashed silver whenever each took
    a step. They could not say what it was they carried—
    perhaps the dream of a child they might bear,

or what it was they hoped to engender in one another.
They knew this as gift, as blessing, as the long-sought
and now-befallen. They simply stepped carefully,
so as not to wake a sleeping god.

Faith

Christine shows me her colored Xerox of an icon,
    the Virgin and Child,
the infant who looks like a tiny man ringed with a halo
    flat as sliced steel,
and I say I cannot see an extra-human love existing,
    and yes, I agree,
a hundred persons cherishing the same ideals
    contain more power
than a solitary soul, an island of single-minded passion.
    We are talking
about church and art, although neither of us says so.
    She says, at least.
I can pray. At least I can write, I don't say, both of us
    casting about
for a possible path around the crossed swords of circumstance
and helplessness that obstruct us—the friend or child intent on
self-destruction, the boss who brutalizes with his thoughtlessness,
all the grim accidental and tragical forces of this life. She tells me
of the long-awaited child who died, the mutant profligate cells,
    the brain
that plays too many tricks. There are life forms so virulent
    they survive
seven-hundred degrees of heat, so delicate they won't
    endure the night.
That old how-can-you-behold-the-stars-and-not-see-God?
    argument sieves through
this refractory mind—or is it heart?—of mine, but you,
dear friend, with your bright eyes and boundless fortitude,
    you I believe.

The End

He was hurling himself
from tree trunk to tree trunk,
not drunk but blundering,

the trees bare and winter-braced,
heavy clouds lumbering
and tattering in high winds,

a last flash of light slitting
the horizon, its strange gold,
almost orange, lining his body.

He was howling *no no* repeatedly,
the frightful howl of severance absolute
as their bodies began to glide back

into their separate bounds
and the tight orb of his voice that lodged
in her voice, and hers that lodged in his,

began to unroll, a ripping sound
hurling against the high reaches
of pines, the lunatic cawings of crows,

the tiresome indistinct taste that clings
to the roof of a mouth,
a river in a mouth, his screaming,

her turning, footfalls hammering
the frozen ground. Four lives
at stake now, and his wife that morning,

naked, in a fetal curl on the rug
beside their bed, her beauty
marred by days of weeping.

What studied blindness guided them?
What animal leap-up of something
ordinary and predictable

had degraded them both? Now each
clutched a longer list of sins
of commission, sins of omission,

the frayed paper of impoverished
imagination, and more invidious scenes
would shine in the nickel-plated hours

of disloyal love, the ploy
of compelling the other to grow
by sacrificing safety, that splintering ruse.

The Speaker

The person who speaks from the center of a field
is a woman whose eyes have been transformed—
one eye a mirror and the other an abyss—

she speaks of the storms that cause clouds
to collide, of thunder, lightning, and the down-
pour of rain; she speaks of the shrill winds

that carve drifts of snow, fling hail and ice
against her cloak and face. She speaks of dark
and of cold, of that infinite vortex that fills half

her gaze, and of the spellbinding charms of colors
and shapes that glance off her mirroring eye.
This woman with the altered and horrifying vision,

sees only extremes. She looks inwardly
on the maelstrom that crazes a soul. She gawks
outwardly on the splendor and squalor of our world.

Yet there is no balance in what she knows—
an uncanny woman in a harsh circumstance.
Never glance at her face nor listen to her voice.

Her eyes will dazzle and distract you, the ululations
of her voice enchant you. Afterwards, you will be
turbulent, frenzied, weep with unbounded despair—

you will practice strange science and the mercurial arts.

Apples

I live near orchards, but only once stole an apple and it was
    windfall—
a Cortland. When I bit into it, snow and blossom, bitter first fruit
and ripe harvest flickered by like light flashing off the windows
of a passing train. There's no word for a bite of apple,
but it doesn't taste like blood. My one ritual on Sunday mornings
from September through February, is to fry sliced apples
with raisins and walnuts, cinnamon, nutmeg, allspice.
Allspice is not made of all spices—it bears a deceitful name.
I roll the fried apples in thin German pancakes, also called blintzes,
spread sour cream on top and pour a ribbon of the maple syrup
I buy from a syrup shack in Pomfret—my town's name sounds
like it means *worried apples*, but it's just a name. For six weeks,
beginning in March, sap boils down in huge vats, steam slipping
from vents and sliding off into the woods. I hum with happiness
when I first see those lidded buckets hooked on the sugar maples,
the first and truest sign of spring. Slicing apples I see moons—
first, full, third-quarter, new—and remember apple pies;
my grandmother peeling, red coil of the skin spiraling from
her hands past the fleshy underside of her white arms,
the dropped coil's collapse to a circle. My grandfather
made applejack the way, he said, the Iroquois made it—
he let the hard cider freeze, then pried off the frozen top.
Hard is a sneaky way of saying half-fermented, so children
won't know you're talking about liquor. Completely fermented
means vinegar. No one grows Baldwins anymore—the trees
are too tall to pick profitably. The apple pickers might fall
from their long two-pointed ladders and sue the orchardist.
We live in a litigious age. Apples are picked from the backs
of pick-ups and only trees with low heavy-bearing limbs
are grown—mostly Macouns, Cortlands, McIntosh.
Winesaps and Jonathans have the deepest plum-rose color,
and Russets are a honey-rose, quite comely, but not the Roxbury
Russet—it looks more like a crabapple. Rhode Island Greenings
are best for baking, but it's easier to find Granny Smiths. I see
a tiny woman under a blooming horse chestnut. She sits deep

in a green Adirondack chair and someone, probably a son-in-law, arrives and helps her stand. Then she walks back to the clapboard farmhouse. Kindly and sweet, Granny Smith makes us think of an America that no longer exists. Golden and Red Delicious are pleasingly shaped, bulging at stem end and tapering down to a five-pointed pucker at blossom end. The orange-red Sheepnose is longer than the Delicious and shaped as its name suggests. The apple with the loveliest name is the Westfield Seek-Me-Not, although some say Cox Orange Pippin is lovelier. I like the striations on the Northern Spies and Wolf Rivers, the chubby rounded shape of the Gravensteins. Everyone knows the opportunistic snake, and not the innocent apple, tempted Eve and caused all of us to dread mortality and feel shame. Her sin too, occasioned labor pains, *travail* the Bible calls it, the consequence I resent most. I understand the apple part—so irresistible. Imagine seeing only one, bending a bough, ready to drop? The apple is the fruit Aphrodite cherished most, and so honored despite Eve's luckless seduction of Adam. Some say the fruit was really Eve's genitalia. Others say every apple is a woman's womb. Wombs do swell and open and issue forth humankind who scatter seed upon the ground. What's best about an orchard is walking through one when no one's spraying. In December, a pruned-back tree holds its grey limbs up to the grey sky; the buds are a hundred nipples growing icy cold. Apple wood sings in fire. If you listen to its high-pitched whine, you hear the deep despair the branches felt when severed from the trunk, an arboreal keening on the air.

Leaving Lovers

He or she is there and you know in the next half-minute
that loved face, body, manner of speaking and moving,
and the precise intensity of beholding you in *those eyes*
will vanish, and you must let all glide into the memorial
past which alone will extend itself into the spaces
the other filled so voluminously. Sometimes you tell
a lie, because you can only face the scene cushioned
by a shallow form of hope. Perhaps the other believes
the dark time is behind now, but this is the downward
slope of love, the chill back corner, the place of absolute
dissolution. Christ, it is never easy, whether the truth
stands unfolded and dissected, or one or both of you is
self-deceived. Perhaps we always know when a parting
is upon us and the light of the next world floods back
onto the world already dissolving, a tainted light
and then a weeping—subaudible but in the air
nonetheless—as if a bell jar stood before us with
the dream of love as an alabaster city or a sylvan glade,
and then some force strikes it with a cosmic mallet,
terrestrial, aerial, tidal, and that is it. It is gone.

Vermeer

The compositions flare toward us as if arrangement
    were a gambol he especially enjoyed,
        but I am drawn to what he uses in painting

after painting: a yellow satin jacket with ermine trim,
    a strand of pearls that end in yellow ribbons,
        a blue and red tapestry he smoothes

across a desk or table or pushes into furrows to ridge
    light in parallels he reinforces in the angle of an arm,
        the edge of a painting, the ledge of a shelf.

He paints in his globe of constellations, and another
    that depicts the known world; on the wall a map of
        The Netherlands flanked with views of Delft,

outdated even then, but there, we suppose, to bring
    fame to his country and city. Vermeer's women,
        except for maids, read and write letters,

drink wine, balance scales, smile and laugh, and play
    guitars, harpsichords, lutes; some are weeks
        from childbed. He loves a luminous face,

beatific, almost always young. Ribbons or jewels
    weave through braids; one woman wears a turban,
        another a red hat, and when he paints Clio,

the Muse of History, she's dressed in royal blue, crowned
    with laurel. He savors the instant someone stands
        transfixed because a perception has opened

what Arnold calls *The Hidden Life.* Imagine, in the middle
    of the seventeenth, mid-morning at that northern
        latitude, walking across the black and white

marble that diamonds his floors, then turning toward
   a window, its light muted by thick leaded glass.
      In each work, the expressiveness of paint,

delicate glazes, thick impastos, linear perspective,
   the subtlety of colors, resolve in an intense suffusion,
      rich with inference, unhampered by time,

a surface where the physical and the metaphysical
   commingle, as in ordinary existence, the interactions
      that are domestic life vanishing in their seamlessness.

Death Is A Material Flower

If you lived in Pomfret, my mother, you would be
forever buying antiques and knickknacks in Putnam,
although you'd sell them soon enough, and for a profit.
I think of you more often than rain comes, and in
unlikely places, you who are ashes for thirteen years.
You traded your life in compromises, not unlike this
lines-for-life trade I make, but death would hedge no bets.
The flowers that bloomed in your heart were pale blue, ·
cocklebells you called them, foxglove, digitalis;
but rosettes crowded your lungs, rosettes rooted in tar
as black as the two-feet deep stoneless soil of Illinois.
In Florida, chameleons scampered like maniacs, then
with a jerk, froze to stone on trunks of palms, along
clotheslines, clothes that would dry in an hour in that hot sun.
Steam and fire, neighbors quarrelling night long, the chafed
smell of St. Augustine grass, palmettos, hibiscus; exotic flora
of last years. Too close the air, or sealed-off entirely,
the world a mirage beyond blinded windows. Here,
heavy lumbering clouds blow in from the Sound,
bring a grey pallor to snow-covered ground, the ground
of bodily unmaking. Stark grief dotted with plastic flowers.
I visit the cemetery because you are gone, but I will not
unspool your death, your death that rose up slowly
and over long years, that clung about your bathrobe
and hair and skin, breath polished to a briny frost.
But Mother, I buy commemorative dolls and plates,
Hummel figurines and carnival glass in your honor,
save silver-plated souvenirs from Algiers and Athens,
from three world's fairs and the Crystal Palace Exhibition,
treasures to loose envious cries from your bridge club,
to fill curio cabinets in the countless corners of heaven.

"Every Man Whose Soul Is Not A Clod Hath Visions"

Between Taylorville and Mattoon, along a flat
numbered country road, hundreds of martin houses,
hotels, motels, apartment buildings, some carved
out of gourds, but most plywood, cut, assembled
and painted to resemble their larger counterparts,
except for the circled entrances and *porches*
the farmer called them. Working at it nearly
thirty years, he said. His kids and grandkids
made some, and folks were always dropping by
with homemade or rescued additions. Vacant usually,
wind-blown as all else on that open prairie,
a town atop poles and hung from trees, strung
along a propped-up beam that ran from milk barn
to hay barn, another from hay barn to tractor barn.
Several accommodations bowed an old clothesline.
Gives you something to look forward to, he said,
those first weeks in April when everyone's moved
in and it's noisy as hell. Each year there's a dozen
or so circling about that can't find a vacancy—
means I've got building to do after the corn's siloed.
He was squirrelly, sunburnt, a bit of a sprite,
one of those husky compact men who have always
stewarded land. Countless times I've thought of
his town for purple martins, fully aloft, swinging
unvisited in snow or the torrential thunderstorms
that rage through that place, motionless, cracking
in August heat, and thought too, of those clamorous
weeks, every household chirping and settling
at nightfall, rousing itself before dawn, the moiré
against fields and clouds as the martins alternate
quick flaps and glides, spread tails and fan-out
over farmland, rise and sink as currents move.
The peal of silence the day they leave. A serious
man's serious folly invented to serve his mind

and spirit as folly will—excessive, redemptive,
preposterous, the glory of the overdone anyone
of us is capable of, yet usually avoids—and
one thing more for him through the long months
of fallow fields—a wild domesticity drawing near.

The Astronomer's Wife

The top right edge of the nearly-round moon
is ragged and she is trying to remember why.
Moonlight is sunlight reflected and the earth's
shadow falls on the moon, that much she thinks
she knows. But then, axis and spinning, the moon's
orbit around earth, earth's around the sun, and vaster—
sun's orbit around the Milky Way. She knows
he is dismayed with her because she prefers the rooms
of her half-knowledge to the estate of his full
understanding. Like a tourist who dallies along one
street and then another, the paths she can take,
willy-nilly, embellishing, thinking things through,
yield a fabulous pleasure. High and constant
the moon through her windshield as she drives
home late. She knows the moon never thinks
or feels, or means or represents, yet she wants
to keep thinking about its changing shape,
and why it rises or sets in one part of the sky
or another, why late mornings she will see it over
a rooftop or tree, or mid-afternoons, a pale grin
of a moon, a bleached beachstone of a moon.
Why only in winter does its light fall on their bed?
Then she watches his form as he sleeps. And why,
in fall, so huge near the horizon, and orange,
not cream, and then—how quickly!—it grows smaller,
whiter as it climbs, the same mass in a different place?
She does not want his answers. She wants her questions.

In Brightest Light

In these early street scenes of London, the passersby
   are unaware photography's taking place.
They are about their business, talking two abreast,
   crossing while watching for cab or tram.

Two women window-shop before Spiers & Ponds, Clothiers.
   A man leaves Hatchard's with a book.
A few lean against wall or post. Each as insubstantial
   now as their shadow was then, and each

with a shadow, since this technique, invented two years
   after Victoria assumed the throne,
requires full daylight. This London's never overcast
   or fogged-in, a city without night,

a place of motion perpetually still. A woman lifts
   her skirt about to step off a curb onto Tottenham
Court Road. We can imagine she will cross Oxford to Charing
   Cross, glance at advertisements as she walks—

signs painted on the brick buildings coming into view.
   She notes the names of establishments
etched in glass doors or brass plates, or painted round
   the flaps of awnings—a look of concern

and a livelier pace after the clock on Magnus Martyr.
   Smell of horse dung steaming on cobbles,
smoke curdling up from blackened chimney pots,
   leather straps slap hides, horses neigh, clop by.

A woman drags a truculent child across Ludgate.
   He pleads and whines, tugs her back intent
on some trinket he would buy. Everyone long dead.
   Another century's come and is about

to slip out of sight as easily as this one has, subsumed
in those productions of time Eternity's
so in love with. A railway caterer's, the British and Foreign
Bible Society, Church of St. Mary Aldermary.

As seamless as the scenes we flow into and out of,
these persons were flooded with clear various
perceptions, their lives as sensate as ours, as they
walked into the greengrocer's or chemist's,
entered Old Blackfrier's Station for the train home.

West Of Tucson

They were waiting at an Exxon for a turn at their
respective johns when he said he'd lick the soles
of her boots if she'd save him from his sinful ways.
Then he suggested a sexual act. She laughed and said
she'd more likely break into German lieder, but that
was lost on him. They were intruded upon by a tall
blond beehived woman weeping wildly for her Italian
greyhound who had just expired from heat prostration
in her car. A $3000 pedigree. What does she expect in July,
windows sealed? A tumbleweed scratched against
a dumpster and leapt as if trying to get in. *If I have to
marry you to get you into bed, then, goddamn it, let's
drive to Reno this second.* She saw a dust cloud shape
itself into Jesus' crucified face then begin to weep.
*You'll be crying O God so much you'll think you've died
and gone clear to heaven.* Arizona's flatbed sky has
similar ambitions; it wants to spread each of us out
and do a thing we'll never get over. Each whisker on
his jowly chin was wire-thick in the thin transparent
air, his lips burnt to a bruise. His Buick stank of cow-
hide on the inside. He had him a ranch he said and
six appaloosas that could benefit from a woman's touch.

The Disclosure

I am married to a bureaucrat, a mid-level administrator. Thomas looks like an ordinary man, but he is a contortionist, something I never discuss with my friends. A tradition in his family for hundreds of years, carried here from Armenia. He and his brothers were taught by their father and two uncles. Before we make love he goes through one position or another. His favorite is *The Box Man*. It is rather frightening to witness, the unfolding as much as the folding up; the corner his genitals take, his head pressed into the carpet. I'm terrified he will suffocate, but he will not tumble from one flat surface of himself to another until the square is perfect. Contortion is deeply connected with the erotic in him and so I try to accommodate his need. What is love for, if not this? Still, I am an uneasy witness to *The Crocodile, The Human Grasshopper, Mister Window, The Croquet Mallet,* etc., and more and more I struggle to desire him, and wish, each time he undresses and moves to the middle of our bedroom floor, that I did not carry the burden of audience, the gift of applause.

Memory and Longing

This morning I miss Lough Corrib, its reed-fringed banks,
    the light-silvered ripples made by swans.

I remember the Yellow Flag iris that blooms so profusely
    in its marshes, the cinquefoil and Ragged Robin,

the ruined castle on its eastern bank and the cows,
    with no heed of history, lolling inside and around it.

Once, while I sat on a spoon of sand among thickets,
    two young men, fully grown—not far off—

stripped down and entered the water. Using the sides
    of their arms they smacked and scooped

attacking sprays at one another, twisting and
    turning the way one must to do this with force.

Each volley shimmered. I became, for a moment, Whitman's
    lonesome woman, the one who stays behind a blind

and watches the twenty-eight. These two seemed to me
    as innocent in their play, as those young men

Whitman, the true voyeur, rendered so lusciously.
    I wanted to stay undetected, but they saw me

and swam across the lake, carried on their frolic
    on the far bank. Amazing and grand—

the lake's mist stepping back into marsh and field,
    the morning growing warmer minute by minute,

starlings bobbing the tips of reeds, gulls moiling over
    a school of fish. Today has a clear and delicate beginning—

as did that morning on Lough Corrib, the rivulets and
    glisten on two beautiful men—only I've nothing to pin it to.

Armageddon

From around my lilacs and lilies, in plaid cotton dresses,
two Witnesses—one of those soft-sophistries-of-June days.
Sisters perhaps, they spoke in earnest mild voices of blasphemy
and sordid sins, God's final wrath—a tepid version, over-rehearsed.
I muttered something about how touchy God was to take things
so personally He'd destroy the Earth and almost everyone on it.
They answered by reading from *The Book of Revelation:*
A hammered dust storm pierced with the cries of crazed birds,
chaos and catastrophe, the final battle, grisly and complex.
For an instant, through that sundering light, Armageddon
seemed to swirl around us. Then the more commanding
of the two, asked if I'd thought about the problem of evil.
I thought then of a dear friend's neighbor, who last fall, in Maine,
an October snow quilting the ground, baked her two-year old.
She told the stricken vomiting detective—the mortuary men
scraping off flesh from an oven rack—God had told her
This child is Satan's. She'd prayed, she said, for guidance.
Of course we have milder cases—the vandals who broke into
an elementary school and shot the pets of a fifth grade class—
hamsters, guinea pig—then broke the fish tank, crushed
the frog, battered the turtle against the chalkboard. Little evils.
You know the stories, can fill in the blanks—writ large,
writ small—for no reason or sick reasons, hourly, daily, for fun
or revenge, or in the name of Allah, Christ, the State,
Shiva, Ram. A profound question, I agreed, but did not ask
how it feels to go home after a day of talking divine carnage
to strangers. How sleep knowing the very ones each says
sweet dreams to are even now condemned? Can they brush
aside the Great Conflagration when they make love,
or do flames swirl through a mind as the body dissolves in
that sweet vacancy? Dandelion fluffs from the orchard
drifted between us, impatiens at our feet. I was lost in disbelief,
apostate; they in myth, believers. Was this fear or foolishness
that drove them door-to-door, day-upon-day, trying to alert—

through terror!—the meager 144,000? Debased of meaning
with each retelling, had even this tale lost its bite the way
the news nibbles at our sensitivity until each horror leaves us
hollow? I watched their skirts lap their legs as they walked
down my driveway. Although hot, each wore oxfords,
stockings, a cardigan, and each curled a Bible to her chest.

Disorders

So that imagined half-calorie could not slide its heat inside,
a hundred times a day Diane threw up even her spit,
her vocal cords acid-marred, her raspy voice legacy.
Even now bulimia can return and begin again its rough
clarifications. Laura carried a pillow wherever she went,
her tailbone bruised with no flesh to cushion it.
Driving her to the clinic the day she could no longer stand,
eighty-three pounds and blanking out, we propped her up
so she could see the world she'd pared herself from.
A thin March light strobing her lucent skin. We rubbed
her belly, coaxed it with song, with prayer, but that
shallow bowl between hip bones and ribs never filled.
Allison would not leave the machines and the gym owner
refused to kick her out, so Judith, her therapist,
talked and listened to a skeleton pedaling, a skeleton
stair-stepping, rowing. Five or six hours a day,
Allison worked death to the surface. Medical
historians tell us this scourge has taken many forms:
Simone Weil would not eat because of the Blitz,
because hunger existed, so she died of self-starvation;
St. Theresa, the Little Flower, took her orders
from Christ: *Take no substance into your flesh but mine—*
so a sip of wine, a thin wafer was all that passed her lips;
quick then, when consumption came for her spare frame.
How strange and dazzling it must have been in Napoli,
when girls first got up to dance, then village by village
through the southern provinces, in plazas, groves, rural lanes,
The Tarantella. The wise insisted a tarantula's bite
caused each to rise and dance until she died. How frantic
and lovely—peasant skirts whirling against land and sea,
at dawn, midday, dusk, at night, unstoppable,
relentless as any quest to release spirit from matter,
to be, by every means, less and less our despised selves.
Disease trundles forth its intractable resolve to diminish,
and vomiting, purging, starving, our daughters come round.

Silver Lotus, Golden Lotus

When I first learned about foot-binding I was a child myself,
wandering alone through display cases at the Museum
of Natural History. A human foot, preserved somehow,
on its side so one could see the press of broken toes
into the pad of the foot, a perfect wedge, the consequence
of bindings first applied at three. There's a long history
of the shoes a foot-bound woman wore, called *lotus shoes*,
tiny boots she would waddle along in, removed by her husband
or lover in the first stages of foreplay. Silk brocade over leather,
elaborately decorated with delicate needlework of blossoms,
vines, butterflies; some carved on the bottom side because women,
especially courtesans and prostitutes, were viewed reclining,
and the man would caress the relief on the soles first,
sliding his fingers in and out of flaps he thought of as petals.
Some shoes had a pocket for a cup, so a man could drink
wine while he slowly unwrapped the almost ten-feet of silk
bindings inside the shoes. All of this highly charged, we are told,
and sometimes the bindings were used to tie the woman
in a bondage game. I think of this on days I savor my stride,
walking vigorously, quickly, throwing my arms into their swing,
light-hearted in the heft and thump of hiking boots
or the foot-slapping slide of mules. A girl with a four-inch
foot had *silver lotuses*, the grand prize was a three-inch foot,
golden lotuses, highly erotic, of immense value on the marriage
market. A mother's pride, a daughter's dainty step; no one
dared break with tradition despite the nights a child muffled
her cries of pain in the pillow she was given for this purpose,
a *lotus pillow*; despite the sores and infections, and sometimes
death, caused by the bindings, precisely and ritualistically applied.
All this—because proverbs are true as everyone knows—
bound feet, bound feet, beyond the gate cannot retreat, for this
and the tantalizing fetish favored by men of the upper classes.

11:00 A.M.

Everywhere a full-blown state of affairs.
    Our thoughts persist above and through
    the rattling drone of someone's lawn mower.

Vacationers are on the beach or they have
    already been and now shun the high sun.
    Caregivers have given themselves over

to those in their care; objects brandish
    their particularities and the mechanical
    processes in leaves gurgle chemicals

speedily along networks of cellulose veins
    making new leaves, blossoms, seeds.
    The big chore of the day is underway.

Its urgent need to be done pounds tiny
    steel hammers against our temples.
    It is almost time to long for late afternoon

or early evening, for a thunderstorm to rumble in
    and disperse the threatening mob of tasks
    mounting the airy staircase of our busyness.

I have not spoken to you in hours but know
    you have thought of me at least twice,
    as I have thought of you.

Here is the thing about love at 11:00 a.m.;
    it steadies the hand and bridges the deep
    crevasses of indecision we must cross

so that what needs to be done, gets done,
　　and who needs to be comforted, is comforted,
　　for accomplishment and peace await us

when the fiery torch of this day is doused
　　and even the night-loving man who roars
　　his mufflerless motorcycle through

our village streets has gone home to dream.

Making Love

1   The Widening

Something like diving into clear water, although not
as exact, launching our tenderest selves beyond
ourselves, losing boundaries, falling away from
what it was we were elsewhere for. The echo of laughter
moving into the canyon, when, leaning over the rim,
we spy tourists on mules spiraling down to the brown
river that slices its bed in two. Are we moving downward
or upward or simply closer? Are we growing diffuse
or more focused? This feeling of welcoming spends us.
One welcomes another into the body, welcomes
the body's deepest wish. We will widen until we vanish.

2   The Entering

Not this alone. Not this unbidden. We have crossed
into the realm no one innocent transgresses, land
of Baptist hymns and maneuvers. Daft and gloating,
jubilant and floating. We are lickingly clean.
Lickingly sweet. Pull back the star-shaped petals
of the mountain laurel until the stamens spring
pollen into the air. Always we were meant to be here,
this journey begun in the womb. Is this shell a nautilus?
Has the clamshell's edge cut our fingers yet? Who
holds the queen conch to our ears? Is this the Atlantic
or the Pacific? Sunset's ambered streaks, a sleek parting
of grey clouds, gold-lit gulls gliding over opaline water.

3   The Removal

The woman who yearns for a child of her own, hands
the newborn back to his mother. This soldier's not going
home, his leave's cancelled. A stranger approaches—
we think?. . . . oh no . . . he's not who we ached to see.

Raining for days and it will rain for days. Crestfallen.
The next ten waves are not as grand as the waves
just crashed, the sea spray's turning briny in our mouths.
And yet something's swirling and tumbling, someone's
beginning to call. A good man carries us home in his car
because we were lost; he departs without leaving his name.
This could be almost pain, almost misfortune.

4   The Revelation

We are married in time but we can part from it. Yes. No.
Who says we cannot go back? How grow into our names?
Is Finland more lovely than Sweden? The answers are pat
but for all that we still lend a hand. Ducks quack and take off,
teal bombardiers. This isn't about what anyone can or cannot
know. Snowing and the grass is dark green, the forsythia
effulgently yellow. February and the Southern Cross
beams its needle radiance into the night sky. What is clear
is astral and floral, mercurial and fleeting, wisdom carnal
and hallowed. Human beings doing these silly perfectly
silly physical things, dying unto ourselves and to no one,
then undying, rehearsing, defying seriousness, rehearsing.

Two Friends Of Mine

I wonder if a profound love lost, is not
like the hard rain that scours these low rocky
hills, a tenacious battering that boycotts
the heart against its healing. Or a mockery
that hides the almost-won, like this immense
white shroud of seaborne fog—the blank hour—
an ungrievable grief. Both wise, intense,
acutely sensitive, finding each other
this side of death was miracle enough, a gift
so seldom bestowed. Not that they denied
the gift, but only could not keep it—bereft
of the place and time required by love's wide
and steadfast promises—he let her go,
she, him, so wife, husband, would never know.

Snowmelt

1

An almost-snowless winter, *brown winter*—
now a late snow freezing as it falls. On the way home,
three high-speed spins on ice, then a slamming pummel.
Snowbank. Dead still in the frozen night.

2

It began in February in the kitchen
when he held his leg against the back of mine.

Snow descends and then melts.
Ablation—the stepping back of snow.

3

Driving to Boston, a windless Swiss dot snow,
a scrim over the story of his heroic youth—
then the longer tale, his marriage's internecine war.

Snowflakes the size of quarters in his hair.
The metallic taste of snow. A flake caught
on his eyebrow. Kissing in snow.

4

Later by the fire, blanket-wrapped, hands
and faces burning. The snow's quiet descent
began as I opened my heart, so much slow
dissolving in a cloud's blank stare, sky breaking up
then savaging itself, white cloak rocking slowly down.

5

Oh Gray-of-the-skies! he would cry—
as if I could disperse and drift over the city.
First step a step into the void. Joy careening into
anguish so fast, the ride ecstatic—but it alters you.
One long spinning skid and life loses whatever
substance kept the parts in place. He's sipping brandy
and smiling at me. He's not going to leave her.

6

Why hadn't I seen the transmutation of sorrow
into charm, self-absorption's outlandish mutations?
A narcissist. That night we took the train back,
all roads closed, again and again the brakes
screeching to a stop—trees fallen on the tracks.
Hungry. Cold. *The city inflated against the dark hover
of infinities . . . drew down to be, in the end only snow.*

7

Only snow! Overhead neon burning all night,
passenger cars smelling of dust and urine.
That storm an anomaly, the way love is an anomaly.

8

Great democratic blanket that descends to hush
and still us. Snow skirling in the wake of his truck.
The last trace of him, the path his tires cut in snow.
After this, I re-made myself, as if I were a blackbird
born on ice. As if I'd killed a fox.

9

Accumulate and ablate. Descend and disappear.

Etymology

The histories of words tell us relationships
compose the world; that *lens* comes from *lentils*
because the first were shaped like the latter;
or that *money* derives from the same word as *mint*,
as in minting coin—words like persons in families
who change across generations and yet stay related.
I trace my first name to that of a river in Scotland
and the people who lived along its banks;
my last name, which means little Jacob, carries me
back to much earlier beginnings, to *heritage*
from the Greek word for *widow*, who,
even these days, stands first in line for *provisions*,
a word that shows provide is connected to *vision*,
as in foresight, and means to care for one's *widow*
because a *husband*, a male who dwells in a house,
should *envision* the misfortunes that might
destroy his lineage, and so make *provision*.
When I aborted the child (*abort* means to be
born badly), I interrupted the line of persons
from that Scottish river and that Hebrew patriarch.
I said, at the time, I have no money and don't
want to marry my child's father, *pater, paternity,*
pattern, patent. I destroyed the future and the child—
no mother from the syllable *ma* that suggests
the burbling of a suckling baby at breast,
ma to *mater* as in *matron* and *matter*, the matter
of a *woman*, from *womb-man*, or *wife-man*,
a man-with-a-womb who is husbanded, a female.

Night Work

Sometimes an immense work is undertaken
that will take months, possibly years to complete.
To refuse this work would consume far more
than surrendering to its requirements,
although they lead to no certain profit.
This is solitary work, yet has a social purpose;
it is honorable, we can trust it. Still it comes
with its price, its delays and digressions
that try our patience. New allegiances
are being forged, hard ground penetrated,
steel rods driven down to anchor a substructure—
the entire construct, the higher elevations—
not yet imagined. When free of daily concerns,
the mind and the body, the spirit turn to this work,
and left to their intelligence, in the ridges
and shallows and streams of unnoticed time,
complete their task, issue their report.
Cataclysm is necessary they tell us, an upheaval,
one that will scatter debris across the existence
we have toiled so long to keep in place.
It is true, as Rilke says, *you must change your life*,
only this time the message is not academic;
it cries out without ceasing, thrusts visions
before our eyes we are forced to perceive,
causes restlessness to race its fiery traceries
up and down our arms, or legs.
Make these choices the work insists, make
them with conviction, make them with haste.

Genius

I dream of the elegant fury of swift thought as it burns
across grey matter like a line of sparking gunpowder
wending toward a cache of dynamite, pure
inventiveness, the grace and pleasure of connections
gathered in a flash and heaved into a vision of possibilities
so dazzling in their combinations they would take a few
centuries to unravel, an inevitable vast architecture
of shimmering design. I've collected descriptions—
my current favorite: *The ability to reconcile the opposing
demands of accessibility and truth,* Grossman's genius.
Reading Dickinson or Dickens, or Joyce, reading Proust,
I'm aflutter, each line blind sided by my wish that I, too,
could do as much. Kurt Gödel was a genius who proved
certain truths are unprovable within the system of logic
in which they are thought. A profound insight that proves
the unparalleled fecundity of the human mind. But Gödel
played his cards close, told few, published little,
was reserved and suspicious, friendless, depressed,
obsessed with his health. Late in life he believed people
wanted to poison him, and when his disabled wife
could no longer cook, he died of starvation,
curled in a fetal position. Gödel's genius could not
bring him joy or love, faith, trust, delight, friends.
Envy is not so much wishing for a thing, as wishing
the other hadn't had it all. A little to rub off. A spreading
round of the right stuff as if a hand could reach into
the genetic pool and broadcast the bright green algae
of scintillate thought, and this has been my sin, to envy
genius as if it were a goodness in and of itself, a gift
devoid of example, disconnected from the whole of life.

The Ideal

As if their very comeliness were centrifugal,
we move back slightly from
the husband and wife standing together
under the outdoor lights of a summer party.
Tanned, vibrant, expressive, perfectly
proportioned, they make clear, unwittingly
and in relief, our ordinary, passably-attractive
selves. What is it like to stand among the less
well-formed, the simply plain with too short
or too long noses, jutting or receding chins
and all the other oddments of contour
and bulk that are the common human lot?
God and goddess, or king and queen, amassing
mythic energy as they speak and gesture,
they are sweet-tempered and thoughtful,
so the sentiment that they exist to diminish
the rest of us, quickly shows itself as jealousy.
We almost expect tragedy to befall them,
they are so unmarred, so near to perfection.
Perhaps they see themselves as less attractive
than they are, know one another's frailties,
foibles, late-night fears, and yet these forms
of model grace—body, face—must astound
and beguile each as they beguile us who relive,
sadly, standing before them, self-conscious
in the light, the long-buried dream we clung to
in our youth: one day we, too, would be beautiful.

Bittersweet

1

A soft drumming of hooves—the deer
turning coat, fleeing the stubble field.
Whitetails rise and sink and rise again,
vanish in the rose-red euonymus
below golden last leaves of maples.
Why do I love November so?
Perhaps an ancient Chinese monk
could clarify the proverbial way
this season and my senses correspond.

2

Whickering lips were skimming chaff
for unharvested cobs, but I've come
for the bittersweet that curls tendrils
through the abandoned apple trees
down slope from this field's far end.
Sometimes driving by I spy a doe
and two not-quite yearling fawns
grazing peacefully, then I dream of
moving deeper into the country.

3

This year *my* woods were subdivided
and four new houses built—yellow,
beige, russet and grey vinyl siding—
each with at least one yappy dog,
now ascatter with pumpkins, potted mums,
seasonal trimmings, cornstalks tied
to porch posts or plopped on lawns—
lost sheaves strayed far from their fields.

4

Next year this field will be lawns,
the bittersweet, if not cut down
with this old orchard, will belong
to someone, not the no one it
belongs to now. I wish the deer,
who look to see if I intend to rob them
of their corn, thick layers of fat
to keep them warm, to keep them
from starving when the snows come—
should they survive the next six weeks
of hunting season, the traffic on this road.

5

Now I see my November nature
derives from loving what I cannot keep,
what will not stay, what lives and dies
or changes when I would have constancy
stave off my darkest midnight thoughts;
misanthropic creature I am becoming,
who would live far away from her kind's
encroachments and silliness. No ancient
Chinese proverb's needed: I am moving
upcountry, beyond my temperate zone.

A Little Charade

Every time I look up a school bus comes down the road. And huge white pieces of the sky keeping falling in chunks on the lawn. The tough part about selling fish is your hands get raw. When we walked into the mist at the end of our tryst, it began to snow. She has an interview in North Carolina and another in Spokane and you know he's not about to change his job. Nothing as lovely as a primordial wood where mosses are ethereal and one sees the past by looking up, the future neatly through the trees. The boom came round and knocked him overboard; they called off the search after thirty-six hours. My mind's a calliope song, or a merry-go-round with canned calliope music. Come with me little Rose, Rosy, Rose-of-Shannon the woman walking through the mall called to her three-year old. Oh Rose. Rose. Neither silence or its bell-clappered duplicate. When she'd been married a year she stopped moving through the world with assurance. Quail eggs around the windfall peaches. A gale tore across the island as if chastening the land. I'm happy to bend down and kiss his forehead and just to see his eyes. The electronic carillon got stuck in the middle of its six o'clock hymnfest; the one long sustained note felt paleolithic. He was a full-time street cleaner and she a full-time woman-of-the-night. Dandelion wine hasn't the color or the taste of dandelions and no one has ever tried to sell it, still I ask when I stop by the spirit shop, "Have you any dandelion wine?" I'm simply going to tell you what the imbecile said: *Forgiveness has teeth and those teeth are unpredictable.* Smiles all around, cascades of smiles. Splendid was her favorite word and then grandeur was and citrine is the stone she wants in her engagement ring. "Events," Durell wrote in Balthazar, "aren't in serial form but collect here and there like quanta, like real life." Her ex-husband grew close to his ex-in-laws and joined their church, later began driving them to their medical appointments. I would not gainsay him for he's the experienced one. *Hat rack, coat rack, give me back my cane*, the children sang skipping rope.

Privacy

I don't want what I say at the end to be made public,
nor what my body may do, how it might spell itself out
with last failings, final strengths. These facts the ether
may keep, the light or its absence in that last room,
and if there is a loved witness, memory's guardian,
then as long as that other lasts—but this alone,
no paper receive the impression, no tape spoken into,
not to relieve grief nor compensate the psyche
for its spirit-companion's banishment. Silence,
silence, and a great opening up are the honor I seek.
Release from time the details and recordable facts.
Unremarkable as this transition is, do not attempt to mark it,
for when the summer grasses come they will etch
their easy erasures, autumn rains will add to the slow
erosion that is the nature of true remembrance,
winds will give their scourings, snows their slow abrasions,
the writing graven on the shifting surface of this earth.

The Beloved's Body

Remarkably real, heightened, larger than . . . .
        more priceless than . . . .
as real, say, as a sculpture of polished steel,
        a Richard Serra, or a David Smith,
or as the Perseids in August hurdling burning
        scars of light,
and, at the same time, more ephemeral,
more motion than substance,
more generosity and curiosity and compassion,
than angles, slopes, or shapes ovate or trapezoidal.

Perhaps there are cities as majestic as his body,
and the meadow I walked through every day
the year I was twenty-two. Most glorious—
the colors of him, the browns and roses and peaches
of him; the way his beard wraps his jaw and chin,
and how it's turned grey from auburn
almost as imperceptibly, as slowly as
        I have aged with him.

Not sternum simply, or the clavicle clarities
        of light, nor the depression
above his buttocks; not his fine soft hair—
the down of human skin—nor his coarser
wiry hair. Earthbound, living, sweet—
fluid, colorful, great thing:
his corporeal, mortal, human form,
the stuff of him, house, hearth, hope of him—
top of crown, tip of toe, guileless, perfect.

Sleeping In

This morning we stretch and stretch our passion
the way you arc your silken back so your skin
can slide free of its shell of sleep. Stay close by me.

I need the rasp and polish of your textures,
and, too, I need the scent of you that rises from
the ground of your true being. What is it opens

and closes and declares itself in your precise timbre?
Do you feel this racy tumult of the heart, as if
tumbleweeds carried us on sand-skimming journeys?

I hear the wind that blows and blows until our
stillpoint holds, dying down as we whirl together
in open-hearted full-tilt spin. Now sing to me.

Your voice soothes like the soft-piling clouds
we see churn after summer storms, the white
vapors billowing higher until struck by sun-gold light.

Perspective

That tiny figure in the distance, an eighth of an inch tall,
is my husband walking back from the ferry,
picking up the groceries ordered from Skibbereen.
He's walking down a serpentine hill that rounds
the harbor wall. Soon he'll vanish as he climbs
the two hills this side of me, then suddenly,
around a hedgerow of blooming blackberry,
fuchsia and grasses, he'll appear nearly full-sized,
smiling, cheerful, holding out the twine-wrapped box
he's carried two kilometers. I like him so close
his face becomes obscured in my near-sightedness,
and at this eighth-inch size as well, his distinct gait
visible even from this distance, so that I can spot him
in a crowd the way a mother sees a child across
several playing fields, in profile, even from
the back and knows its hers. He's known by me,
although, at times, he surprises me as he did
last night when he picked up a rock and smashed
the mortar sealing a farmer's gate latch because
he wanted access to private property, so damaged
property to get it. So out of character, this act,
it's taken me aback. Back to where? To the time
before we came into one another's sphere, strangers.
Perhaps we never know the one we think we know
so intimately, the unpredictable predictably to erupt
and dislodge our preconceptions, the way the heart
of life is erratic and wild, and each of us is autonomous
and free, and I've yet to speak to him of my dismay.

Pregnant

Sometimes I wish I were pregnant again
so I could feel that ridge of pressure pushing
out from under my ribs, touch that taut smooth
bulging dome that sloped down to the pubis
I could no longer see. I liked the way
the steering wheel would glide its half-ring
round and back just below my popped-out navel,
the moored sense of cradling a world inside.
The visitor I transported and fed was restless
as a bee and I enjoyed the delicate flutterings,
then the soft padded kicks and tiny fists
punching inside of me. I liked easing down
into bed, rolling on my side with anchoring
gravity, and in that great balancing act
of walking or going down stairs, I felt
acutely real, new life having filled the void
in which the flimsiest sense of self had tried,
and always failed, to lay its claim.
My vague disappointment disappeared,
and the detached miasma I drifted through,
an existence that had always seemed, before,
likely to fly out the window, or evaporate.
I had someone to be and someone to be for,
and although I was terrified of the helplessness
a woman feels when life's most strenuous force
begins its rending, beyond pain's mitigation,
I was happily huge, joyfully holding.

Ramelli's Reading Wheel

Albertian in its ingenuity, designed so the spirit might triumph
over matter, Ramelli's small ferris suits the scholar with gout,
or any bibliophile who chooses not to move. This fifteenth
century convenience holds, each on its lectern, ten open
books that seem, when the wheel is turned, about to topple
on the reader's head, but the books journey downward
toward the floor, slightly disorienting, but without consequence,
taking the thirsty from the ladle of knowledge to the well,
from what will suffice to that last scattering of knowledge
where all becomes faint and immeasurable. Ninety-two
wedges and glueless joints, all wood, built for the humanist
of Raphael and Leonardo, a figure which exists for the
intersection of square with circle, so the turned wheel
becomes a multiplying circle, the axles rotating accurately,
each book presented suitably angled for the acquisitive gaze.

The Ten Books

1
On the Manufacture of Sails Through the Ages With Appendices
Devoted to the Techniques of Phoenician and Sicilian Shipwrights.

2
The Five Sacred Roles of the Admirable King: Judge, Conqueror,
Master of Servants, Censor and Orderer of the Universe.

3
The Legal Code of Mesopotamia Concerning Wrongful Speech,
Especially in the Cases of Women (Gossip) and Peasants (Slander).

4
The Making of Noteworthy Eunuchs: Training Before and After
Incision, With a Guide to the Stanching of Blood.

5
Our Lady of the Date Palm, Our Lady of Contraptions and Riggings,
Our Lady of Underground Stores: Litany for a Few Lesser Saints.

6

The Painted and Gilded Kayiks of the Bosphorus:
The Ottoman Nobility at Play.

7

Desolate Defiles and Raging Rivers: A Norseman's Travels.

8

Preventing and Treating Saddle Sores in the Livery
While Delousing Vagabonds and Hapless Wayfarers.

9

The Hair Shirt and Other Oddments of Penance.

10

Pirates and Plunderers, Sackers of Cities:
Rapacity at Work in the Modern World.

The architect, Daniel Libeskind, discovered a few years ago
when he built Capitano Agostina Ramelli's wheel, the first
to exist, working with the old tools and by candlelight,
striving *to become the pure medieval craftsman*, Ramelli's drawings
were exquisitely rendered; all parts fit together flawlessly.
My reading machine's a haphazard miscellany of books,
journals, papers, magazines, scattered upstairs, downstairs,
even in the car, and the churring I hear is my cognitive
wheel—that slow reordering and composting of facts
and images that rise up from the surface of the text
to become a reverie, or sleeplessness, the thickening
embroidered tapestry that is the backdrop of a world.
What is a book that it unfolds for us what no other
medium can? Delightful, troublesome, lavish, implicating,
a day or two, a week's desultory reading is not unlike
the sparkling shoals of jeweled fish ornaments
the women of a sultan's harem would drag in chains
behind their excursion boats, the fish fanning out
over the boat's wake, dazzling in their radiant shimmer.
The way the texture of life flickers in the wake of a book.

Irish Holiday

Some fare alone better than others—the widow traveling
with a granddaughter, the man with the broken life,
the shy one who writes Borgesian stories. Back from Iowa
and Italy, she travels only to places beginning with "I"—
India is next. I didn't tell her that when I lost
my mind I'd become entangled in a utopian scheme.
The long walks we took, sauntering, from *santeren*,
to muse or make a holy pilgrimage. Now, under the lindens,
young Irish girls in long skirts, sandals, book bags,
brown and auburn hair blown back. When I was young
I never knew my beauty gave pleasure to the women
who watched me. Sorrow and silence, slate roofs
the color of wind-turned leaves, edged with patinaed
copper. *You haven't got a prayer, I'm sure, all is so indelicate.*
Laughter and embraces and deep soppy kisses—lovers
in the carved arched doorway. Three lean cyclists sit
spread-legged on the hill. *Yes,* I said, *I've been betrayed before.*
The wild look in that mother's eyes, and then later, in the pub,
our lifting one to her boy's health. On the next-over
bench, a woman changes her baby's nappy. We are not
mutable, no alchemical formulas here. All the love
that woman's got, her worshipful legions, yet she holds
what no one seeks, trapped in her thin whiny voice.
On my walk this morning, a calf struggled up, forelegs
then wobbly hindlegs, the maroon and grey placenta
dragging from its center. My augury remiss—
I didn't see an accident coming. Returning first as mist,
a soft day. A recorded pipe song, then a reel. The pleasures
of the reel come with the chord changes. The pleasures of
whitewashed surfaces come against the green, or in fog,
or on clear days, against the blue-white-grey sky. Well,
I won't complain. *I came back looking for you, Darling*, he said.
*Oh no, no, I told him, you're lost. You're looking for someone
else.* I never knew the particular desire to touch but not see.
So easy to spot priests on holiday, even out of clerical garb.
All signs of peace are visible, ripple through the benevolent air.
Now the infant wails its offended wail, shatters the frail light.

Stardust

At the Draw Bridge Inne in Mystic,
   I am sitting where we sat
      and drinking dark beer in your honor,

toasting your gaze as seen here
   on a cold mid-November night a season ago.
      You remember the piano player?

He's singing *In My Imagination*,
   which is where I am right now.
      If you were here you would recall

Louie Armstrong's far better version.
   The French bread is perfect
      and there are fresh beets in the salad.

The first time I came here, a year ago,
   all of us, all of that, hadn't happened.
      Now, for comic relief, he's singing

Back in the Saddle Again. The house dressing
   is a honey-dill vinaigrette. My waiter
      is outlandishly affected, a pretty boy.

I can hear you getting him to talk
   so we can enjoy his very fey voice.
      When you were here, across from me,

I was telling you about my split selves;
   how, humiliated and rejected by my family,
      I had divided myself in two to survive:

my meek and ashamed self
   and my bold show-them self;
      one or the other of me could hide for years.

I was accounting for the double
    messages I'd been giving you
        that you'd been pointing out to me.

Love is now the stardust of yesterday.
    I was trying desperately to keep your love,
        not to tromp on what had moved into

and magnified my life, the lance
    of your spirit. And now I haven't spoken
        to you in a week, and then to say

I didn't think we should ever make love again
    because I get entangled in your subjectivity,
        losing myself and my good sense.

Bye-Bye Blackbird. I don't want to turn
    my life into a story, yet this helps somehow,
        putting a glaze of distance between the memory

of your presence in this very place where you,
    in the delicate wonder of your person, spoke,
        leaned forward, added kindness to the air.

Under The Sign Of Walt Whitman

Whitman would have admired Willimantic's
4th of July Boombox Parade, the most democratic
parade in America, the only requirements—
wear something red, white or blue, show up
and march. *The Stars & Stripes Forever*
is followed by *Anchors Away*, but no one comes
for the music broadcast over W-I-L-I, boomboxes
lining the sidewalks and perched on the ledges
of windows so there's no need for uniforms
and brass bands. Church groups, clubs, proponents
of this-or-that, businesses, bureaus, kids on bikes
and skateboards, dogs, politicians and librarians
all convey themselves down Main Street, so
American you could cry, and of course you do
for the wonder of it, for the glory of the human pageant
and its gift for self-expression, and every possible
American is here, *grande y piqueño*, young and old,
rich, poor and middling. The Rainbow Coalition flares
its colors and The Wild Women of Willimantic
strut their stuff, as does The Precision Drill Team
(marchers holding power drills), The Lawn Mowers'
Brigade, and The Baby Boomers' Unit (child and
stroller required). The Unitarians and The Boxing
Club march, antique car owners glide their gleaming
beauties, and this year six little girls dressed
as teacups for no special reason. The florescent
spiked-hair tattooed and leather-clad baldies show,
and various malcontents, but no cops—they're off
on the side streets directing traffic—for this parade
says fly the flag of your most outrageous disposition
and cry your barbaric yawp over the rooftops
of this old mill town. In this wild, discombobulated
American-style hubbub, we celebrate community
and "the blessing of liberty," we celebrate ourselves.

Irises

Dozens to unearth, cut, dust, replant—
    tall bearded, miniature, Siberian—
ruffled blossoms and the bi-colored
    varieties—purple and cream, deep wine

and lighter wine. The ancient Greeks,
    dazzled by its colors, named it: *iris* means
"eye of heaven"—their word, too, for rainbow—
    and for the colored rim around the pupil

that controls how much light we let in
    our eyes, how much our hearts let out.
I have a photo of a plump middle-aged woman
    (no doubt she's passed on by now), who holds

a pale red-violet iris and smiles proudly—
    her namesake cultivar, Louise Watts.
My grandmother mail-ordered rhizomes
    from her in the fifties, then they corresponded.

Her iris has moved with us through gardens
    in Virginia, Maryland, Massachusetts, and now
flourishes in my Connecticut beds. Over the years,
    I've given Louise Watts to at least a dozen

people, as my grandmother and mother had,
    my aunts and sisters too. When I get around to
this task which weighs on me, I'll have more
    to find homes for—I can't toss them.

The Wattses, George and Louise, devoted
    their lives to irises, grew unnumbered varieties
on an acre in Armonk, New York.
    Surely husband and wife were compelled

and remade by their common undertaking.
If burdened by an overabundance of beauty,
they found a way to go beyond it—
a peaceful unobtrusive way to perpetuate love.

The Wind

During a lull, the woman could close her eyes and sigh, could rest, for this woman felt compelled to feed the wind and believed that without her diligence, her persistence, the wind would slacken and cease to blow through trees and over roofs, cease to spindrift the crests of waves, ruffle the feathers of birds. Cornsilk would lose its sibilance, snows their drifts, and never again would petals skirl the floors of orchards. There were days and nights on end when the wind demanded constant feeding. It would come into her yard with its blank cavernous mouth and she would hurl up straw with a pitchfork. At such times she would grow exhausted and crabby, and feel her heart had been gnawed. Such incessant howling and whistling! It was hard not to rail against the wind, although if she gave into her rage, the wind would turn back and stream into her face. Once, after four days and nights of moans in the eaves and shrieks in the chimney, with all her strength she hurled an old harpoon into a birch. *You've taken everything from me*, she screamed, *everything, everything!*

Equally bewildering were those times when the dank smell of silence leached fear out of the earth and nothing she could read in the signing of clouds comforted her. Stillness, placidity, and vacuousness bleached her thoughts. She would strain to hear that first small teasing suss that is the wind's tongue glazing the rims of leaves. To distract herself she would crown the barn with bales of straw, prayers rattling like pebbles in her mouth. Waiting, listening, fully prepared, she believed that if she must go on unrelieved, pure longing would strip her skin away and she would be raw as a peeled persimmon. No sleep for her on perfectly quiet nights, none on nights of boisterous tossings; no sleep in the church of stillness, no sleep in the coliseum of blow. O there is no passion more infuriating than one for the wind, terrestrial or oceanic, solar or galactic, none more demanding; no force more magnificent, no satisfaction more elusive.

Bones

Bones of a severed hand outstretched, pleading.
The braced-for-a-leap bones of a cat.
Long teeth of the anglerfish that fold down to admit prey,
spring up to prevent escape. Bones of entrapment,
bones of flight, an eardrum that shakes the tiny
auditory ossicles that carry Brahms to me.
I've got bones I want to sell you, bones to make a broth.
Distal phalanges, middle phalanges, the small dog bone-like bones
of the palm. A nest of wrist bones. Give me a hand
and your bones come forth, your extended self,
parts that will outlast you. A bracelet of coiled bones,
boa of the great squeeze, the great gulp, vertebra and rib,
each almost, but not exactly, like the next, shrinking
in size until the thinnest, smallest, at the base of a flat
ovoid skull, at tip of tail. Force, stress, strain, tension,
pressure always, bones bear weight, and like our ribs,
the ribs of canoes, of ships, of tents and houses.
Carry and bear and yet not burden. Bones picked over,
licked clean, smooth or scabrous to the touch.
Bone chill. Bone grinding. A calcified dust.
A current under sea picked his bones in whispers.
Long buried bones. The saint's knuckle bone
in a jeweled case, a monk's in an ossuary, a temple
of bones, a pyramid of skulls. At the concert—
two hundred and six bones in each seat.
The strength of bones matched to the force of experience.
Shattered bones, bleached bones, bonemeal, marrow.
The horn carved of an antler; the fine filtering hairs
on the whale's jawbone. Girders and cables and pulleys
like ligaments and tendons. Levers and hinges like joints.
The spiny lacework of bone cells. The rattlesnake
erects its fangs to strike, a fish extends its jaw
into a long sucking tube—evolutionary novelties—
these mobile bones. We dance jigs because we have bones.
Only bones remain embedded in lava. Flexible, light,
intricate, strong. The arms of the wishbone

as the wings beat up and down. A dime's weight in my palm,
skeleton of a bat found under my desk. The surgeon
drilled a ring of circle holes into the plate of the skull,
tapped on it until it cracked, then lifted off the frontal bone.
Vertebrae of a lion that bend and extend in each galloping stride,
or the spine of any cat, flexing and twisting in different ways
from one part to the next, so the falling cat rights itself
before it lands, unlike leg joints that press one bone
on another so surfaces slide over each other as the joint
moves. My arthritic knees. A femur breaks, a clavicle,
humerus, illium; our joints crack. Where we came from,
where we need to go, our bones journey. Old bones, go slow.
Bones don't break now, don't fracture or splinter or shake.
No life without bones, except of the spineless,
gelatinous sort—bacterial, viral, fungal, moss. No life
to make a work that stands. Although some praise the heart,
others the brain, some the tongue or eye, I praise what remains
when all else rots—and the white shard that flecks the ash.

A West Cork Suite

1

Crevices and curls of stone and the mortise-
fallen holes the wind's tongue probes
makes it clear this place is the wind's
best hope of sounding out its changeable mind.
The blue-green and yellow-green grasses
are foils for the wind's confidence games,
so easily splayed, swirled, twisted, and when
rain-heavy, laid flat. Yet every hour across
the sky, new pleats of quiet unfold.
One feels the descending peace, until,
truly, *peace comes dropping slow*—then
a gull's cries tatter it. Once today I heard a gull
bark, another mew, and still another laugh—
gulls of updrafts, tide-dipped, wimple-winged,
swift-banking cliff climbers. And the pheasant
foraging the west field, his drab self-effacing
hen ten pheasant-paces back, his calls scratchy
and shrill, he's a creature easily annoyed,
dyspeptic. In the night, a wail like a child abandoned
on the cliffs, and a low whimpering that's got me
guessing this stone house is haunted. I close
the curtains. The tight-lipped heather murmur,
bunch against the wind's regaling ballyrag.

2

Since there's no drainage in a bog, only black
water trickling from crevices of rock, you can climb
higher through the furze and heather and the ground
gets wetter—or no drier. Peat, crushed or slated
shale, chunks of quartz, grasses tufted or goat-cropped,
the bracken and gorse salt-laced, wind-blasted.
The dead of it all stacked and packed, compounded
thirty thousand years, plus outcrops of rocks scattered
about as if they had been scarves the wind caught,
carried, dropped. The force field of a bog draws
us in, electrifies us, the way we might feel holding

a lead pellet that had been, eons earlier, a gaseous planet,
the agelessness of this terrain proclaiming
our status among the living as horrifyingly brief—
we are on the ground, and then we are of it.

3

It is raining on the clothesline clothes,
an Irish laundry, the kind one hangs
on Monday, takes down on Friday, in a country
where time is green and lime deposits bleed
toward the surface of stone. *It's not easy to feel
cheery,* she said, the sky battened down for days,
it weighs on you. Weather like charity gone wrong,
like justice miscarried. The Cork mountains have
vanished, the sea's vanished, only a woman's thigh
and hip and waist of a hill stays visible, and
a brightly-painted cluster of holiday cottages
that cater to themselves. The cows are soaked.
Annie's blue nightgown's soaked. Lichen
have finished polishing their silver service
which they display so broadly on the stones;
the copper-patinaed filigree of mosses swell.
In the lulls, the complaints of hooded crows
sounding perfectly ecclesiastical. No one strays far.
Soft sorrow of skies, a muddle of clouds, a rumble of sea.

4

This is not my place, nor these my people;
not these two-stepping a waltz to mandolin,
violin and concertina, then later, two girls
with bodies firm as cedars step-dancing,
arms held high and joined, two impassive
flat expressions that signal concentration.
Jewel-buds of youthful faces, rose-cups
of older faces, the music ranges from reels
to zydeco, and the feeling is comfort,
earthbound, warm, home-folk purchased,

what we do best with our social selves;
drink, laugh, flirt, make music, dance.

5
The thrift is blooming in tumbles and falls
down the walls near South Harbor.
One knows to call the foxglove and ox-eye daisy
flower, but what of the lanky dandelion that
opens its small Aztec suns over the flagstone
path, or the elder that blooms by the road?
Here, distinctions slink-off into the vaporous
distances . . . . The sudden thwack of a fulmar
flying near the house, the long laments
of two cows commiserating two fields apart,
galleries of sounds opening one onto another
and I have yet to find the guard who knows
the closing hour, while a small blue boat,
red-trimmed, rocks in the harbor that glows
variously green, grey, aquamarine, cerulean
and all gradations in between. It rows nowhere,
belongs perhaps to Kitty, the horse, who watches
over it from her wild highland meadow,
dragging over the damp bracken and gorse
the long blue rope of her eventual breaking.
Here—like looking deeply into an opal—
there are sights mercurial and serene,
a secret-keeping, secret-yielding arabesque
of shadows moving in-and-out of light,
the kaleidoscopic harvest of the deliriously still.

Notes

"Emily" is for Emily Walpole.

"Faith" is for Christine Czajkowski.

"Leaving Lovers" is for Honor Moore.

The title "Every Man Whose Soul Is Not A Clod Hath Visions" is taken from the first stanza of John Keats' "The Fall of Hyperion."

"In Brightest Light" derives from my study of the photographs collected by Peter Jackson and published in *Walks in Old London*, Barnes & Noble Books, New York, 1993.

I learned about "Silver Lotuses, Golden Lotuses" from *Shoes: A Celebration of Pumps, Sandals, Slippers & More*, by Linda O'Keffe, Workman Publishing, New York, 1996.

The quoted lines in "Snowmelt" are Robert Penn Warren's from his poem "Answer to Prayer." *Selected Poems: 1923-1975*, Random House, New York.

"Night Work" is dedicated to Ahmayo Bohm and Margo Tabb Summerfield. The quoted line is from Rilke's poem "Archaic Torso of Apollo."

The allusion to Grossman's definition of genius in "Genius," derives from the fol-lowing statement of Allen Grossman's found on p. 111 of *The Sighted Singer*, The Johns Hopkins University Press, 1992: "The making of poems always involves a conciliation of the competing claims of accessibility, on the one hand, and truth on the other. The capacity to conciliate these severely antagonistic claims is, in my view, virtually the same as the genius which is poetic."

Daniel Libeskind wrote about Ramelli's Reading Machine in *Countersign*, 1992. *Le diverse et artificiose machine del Capitano Agostina Ramelli* was first published in Paris in 1588.

The story about George and Louise Watts mentioned in "Iris" comes from *Perennials* by James Underwood Crockett and the Editors of Time-Life Books, Alexandria, Virginia, 1972.

"Bones" derives in part from my study of the photographs and text of *Bones: The Unity of Form and Function* written by R. McNeill Alexander and photographed by Brian Kosoff, A Peter N. Nevraumont Book, MacMillian, USA, 1994.

Gray Jacobik, winner of the 1997 Juniper
Prize for her book of poems *The Double Task*
(University of Massachusetts Press, 1998),
has published three other collections of poetry:
Sandpainting (1980), *Paradise Poems* (1978),
and *Jane's Song* (1976). An NEA fellow, her
work has appeared in *The Kenyon Review*,
Ontario Review, *Alaska Quarterly Review*,
Midwest Quarterly, *Connecticut Review*, *Prai-
rie Schooner*, *Southern Humanities Review*,
North American Review, and *Georgia Review*,
among others, and her poems have been pub-
lished in a number of leading anthologies, in-
cluding *The Best American Poetry, 1997* and
1999. Professor of Literature at Eastern Con-
necticut State University, she lives in Pomfret,
Connecticut.